World At Risk

WASTE DISPOSAL

Andrew Solway

FRANKLIN WATTS

LONDON•SYDNEY

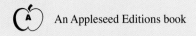 An Appleseed Editions book

First published in 2009 by Franklin Watts

Franklin Watts
338 Euston Road, London NW1 3BH

Franklin Watts Australia
Level 17/207 Kent St, Sydney, NSW 2000

© 2009 Appleseed Editions

Appleseed Editions Ltd
Well House, Friars Hill, Guestling, East Sussex TN35 4ET

Created by Q2AMedia
Editors: Katie Dicker
Art Director: Rahul Dhiman
Designers: Harleen Mehta, Ritu Chopra
Picture Researcher: Shreya Sharma
Line Artist: Sibi N. Devasia
Colouring Artist: Aadil Ahmad
Technical Artists: Abhideep Jha, Bibin Jose, Manoj Joshi

ISBN 978 0 7496 8810 3

Dewey classification: 363.72'8

All words in **bold** can be found in the glossary on pages 42–43.

Website information is correct at time of going to press. However, the publishers cannot
accept liability for any information or links found on third-party websites.

A CIP catalogue for this book is available from the British Library.

Picture credits
t=top b=bottom c=centre l=left r=right
Cover Images: Shutterstock: bg, Inset: Sean Gladwell/Shutterstock: cl, Andreas Gradin/Shutterstock: c, Shutterstock: cr.

Ravike Concepts/ iStockphoto: Title Page, Sean Gladwell /Shutterstock: Content Page, James Leynse/Corbis: 8, Stephen Aaron Rees/
Shutterstock: 10, Russell Shively/Shutterstock: 12, Bruce Works/Shutterstock: 13, Bob Sacha/Corbis: 14, Michael Goossen/Shutterstock: 15,
Vadim Kozlovsky/Shutterstock: 16, Douglas Peebles/Photolibrary: 19, Ravike Concepts/iStockphoto: 20, Michael S. Yamashita/Corbis: 21,
Finbarr O'Reilly/Reuters: 22, Brandon Seidel/Shutterstock: 23, RBR/Photolibrary: 24, Alexis Rosenfeld/Photolibrary: 25, Bruno Domingos/
Reuters: 26, SPL/Photolibrary: 27, Sally/iStockphoto: 29, Mick Rock/Photolibrary: 30, Shutterstock: 31, John Linden: 32,
Lester Lefkowitz/Photolibrary: 33, M Govarthan/The Hindu Images: 34, Kevin Britland/Shutterstock: 35, William Manning/Corbis: 36,
Amit Bhargava/Corbis: 37, Bernard Bisson/Sygma/Corbis: 38, Stillfx/Shutterstock: 39.
Q2AMedia Art Bank: 9, 11, 17, 18, 28, 41.

Printed in China

Franklin Watts is a division of Hachette Children's Books,
an Hachette UK company.
www.hachette.co.uk

CONTENTS

1

MOUNTAINS OF WASTE

What would it be like if everything you have ever thrown away came back to haunt you? There would be thousands of cans, tonnes of paper and hills of rotting food.

Earth Data

- Americans throw away 60 million plastic bottles every day – 694 a second.

- The average college student produces 300 kg of waste a year, including 500 disposable cups and 145 kg of paper.

- In open-pit copper mining, about 99 tonnes of waste is thrown away for each tonne of copper produced.

How much waste?

Our modern lifestyles generate literally mountains of waste. Each year around the world, we produce about 1,200 million tonnes of waste from homes and offices. That's enough to fill 30 million heavy trucks. **Construction** and mining produces even more waste – enough to fill 180 million trucks every year. Then there is waste from factories, farms and **sewage**.

> This landfill site on Staten Island, New York, USA, used to be the biggest in the world. When it shut in 2001 it was taller than the Statue of Liberty.

Waste generated around the world

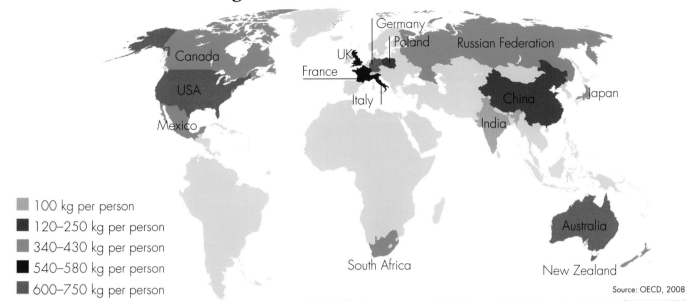

100 kg per person
120–250 kg per person
340–430 kg per person
540–580 kg per person
600–750 kg per person

Source: OECD, 2008

This map shows the total waste generated per person each year in 15 different countries of the world.

Where does our waste go?

Much of the world's waste is buried or simply dumped untreated. **Landfill sites** are particular areas where our rubbish is buried. But landfill sites are filling up and new sites are increasingly hard to find. Even when landfill sites are full and covered over, they must be monitored for many years to avoid leakage and **pollution**. The waste is buried underground but it could cause problems for future generations.

Other waste is burned or thrown into the ocean. Whatever method we choose, getting rid of waste creates all kinds of problems – and these problems vary in different parts of the world. In more economically developed countries (**MEDCs**), there are well-organised systems for collecting and disposing of rubbish. But these countries produce a lot of waste. Today, more waste is being generated than can be dealt with. People in the USA and Norway, for example, produce nearly eight times

as much waste as a person in India. People in MEDCs consume more – they buy more things and when something breaks, they are more likely to throw it away than fix it or reuse the materials.

Less economically developed countries (**LEDCs**) produce less waste per person, but have other problems to deal with. This is because many cities in LEDCs have grown very quickly, and the sewage system and the waste disposal system cannot cope. One city in Kenya, for example, produces about 33,000 tonnes of waste each year, but only 6,600 tonnes are collected. The result is piles of rubbish in the streets, streams blocked with waste and landfill sites that are a serious health hazard.

The world is at risk from the waste we produce. We cannot continue to generate this much waste and dispose of it as we are doing today. This book looks at the problems of the waste we generate, and ways of changing how we deal with it.

2

WHAT WASTE DO WE PRODUCE?

On average, each person in Europe produces about 550 kilograms of waste each year, and the figures are even higher in the USA. So what exactly are we all throwing away?

Household waste

A lot of our household rubbish is made up of food or plant waste. Garden waste (such as weeds and grass cuttings) and waste food make up nearly 40 per cent of household waste. In the UK, for example, about a third of the food that people buy ends up in the rubbish bin. Newspapers, magazines, envelopes, leaflets and packaging are another huge part of our waste. When we buy goods, they usually come in a box, a can, a carton or a bottle. This packaging is mostly made up of cardboard, plastic, metal or glass and is invariably thrown away.

About 60 per cent of all **commercial waste** is paper or cardboard of some kind. There is also a surprising amount of food. About a fifth of all the waste from offices, shops and schools is unwanted food.

Household waste is stored in bins or bags so it can be collected for disposal.

Composition of household waste

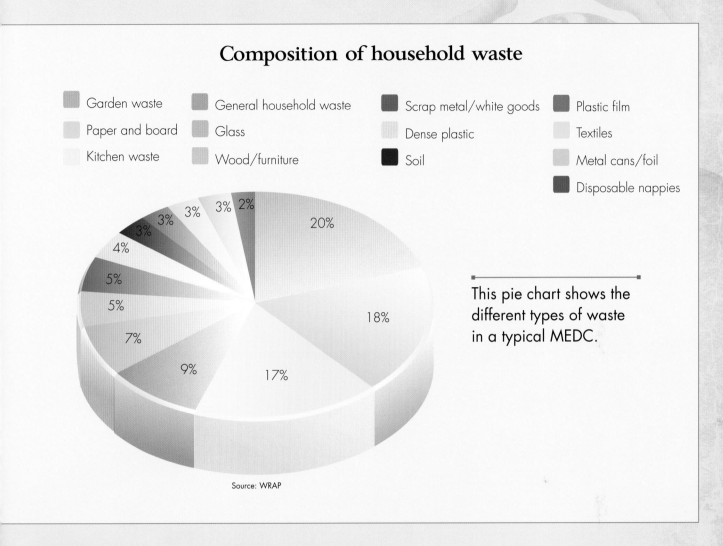

■ Garden waste   ■ General household waste   ■ Scrap metal/white goods   ■ Plastic film

■ Paper and board   ■ Glass   Dense plastic   Textiles

Kitchen waste   Wood/furniture   ■ Soil   ■ Metal cans/foil

■ Disposable nappies

This pie chart shows the different types of waste in a typical MEDC.

Source: WRAP

Differences between countries

While MEDCs and LEDCs produce different amounts of waste they produce different types of waste, too. In general, LEDCs use far less paper and cardboard than MEDCs. This is because fewer people work in offices or other places that use paper products. People in MEDCs use, on average, over 2 tonnes of paper and cardboard a year. It takes over 500 trees to produce this much paper and card for each person.

In LEDCs, people also throw away less cardboard, plastic, metal and glass because they buy far fewer packaged goods. In towns or villages, goods are often bought in markets. In remote regions, there may be no postal services requiring parcels and packaging. Instead, up to 80 per cent of rubbish is food or plant waste.

11

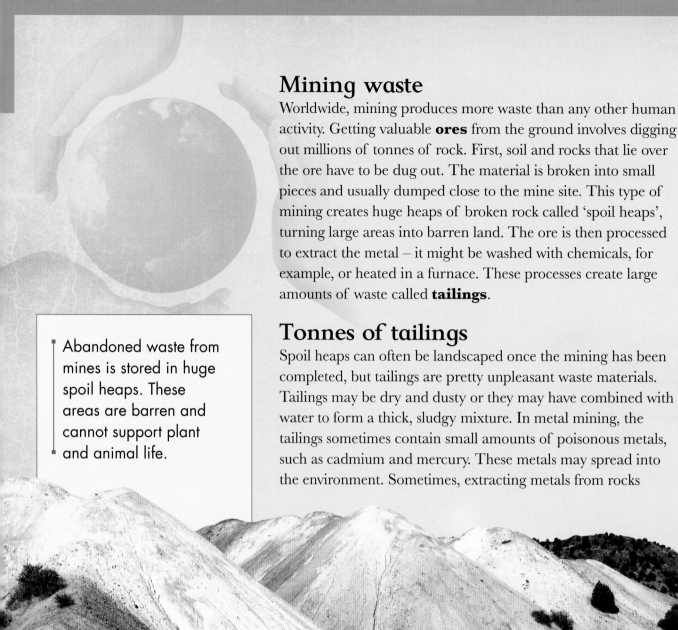

Mining waste

Worldwide, mining produces more waste than any other human activity. Getting valuable **ores** from the ground involves digging out millions of tonnes of rock. First, soil and rocks that lie over the ore have to be dug out. The material is broken into small pieces and usually dumped close to the mine site. This type of mining creates huge heaps of broken rock called 'spoil heaps', turning large areas into barren land. The ore is then processed to extract the metal – it might be washed with chemicals, for example, or heated in a furnace. These processes create large amounts of waste called **tailings**.

Tonnes of tailings

Spoil heaps can often be landscaped once the mining has been completed, but tailings are pretty unpleasant waste materials. Tailings may be dry and dusty or they may have combined with water to form a thick, sludgy mixture. In metal mining, the tailings sometimes contain small amounts of poisonous metals, such as cadmium and mercury. These metals may spread into the environment. Sometimes, extracting metals from rocks

Abandoned waste from mines is stored in huge spoil heaps. These areas are barren and cannot support plant and animal life.

involves the use of some very dangerous chemicals. Extracting gold, for example, may require the use of the deadly poison, cyanide. The resulting tailings often contain **toxic** chemicals. Millions of tonnes of tailings have been produced every year for many decades. If we do not dispose of this waste safely, mining land will be unfit for use for hundreds of years.

Construction waste

Building work also produces a lot of waste. Even a small building job can fill a large skip with old plaster, broken or rotten wood, bricks, tiles and other materials. Larger construction projects, such as skyscrapers and dams, create thousands of tonnes of waste. Sometimes, construction waste includes new materials. On a large project, it can be difficult to order the right amount of materials. For large building companies, it is often cheaper to throw these leftovers away rather than collect, sort and find alternative uses for them.

PLANET WATCH

» In 2002–3, 107.5 million tonnes of construction and demolition waste was created in the UK. This was a whopping 71 per cent of all UK waste.

» In 2004, about 119 million tonnes of waste was generated in Sweden. Around 58 million tonnes of this was mining waste, while building and construction accounted for 10 million tonnes.

The waste produced by the construction industry each year is about three times the total amount of household and commercial waste.

Other industries

Some types of industrial waste can be dealt with in a similar way to household rubbish. However, many industries produce hazardous waste. This is waste that is toxic, **flammable**, **infectious** or **radioactive**.

Oil refineries, power stations, iron and steel mills and chemical factories are among the largest producers of hazardous waste. This waste needs to be made safe, or stored securely. Sometimes, hazardous wastes, such as liquid wastes from the chemical industry, are burned to get rid of them safely. Most solid waste is stored – in strong containers, special landfill sites or in storage sites deep underground. This keeps the waste safely out of sight but does not remove it completely. This waste could be a problem for future generations.

E-waste

E-waste is a term used for all the computers and other electronic equipment that people throw away. Around the world, we get rid of up to 50 million tonnes of e-waste every year – that's more than a tonne of e-waste a second. The amount of e-waste is also growing about three times faster than other kinds of waste.

Computers and other electronic equipment contain valuable materials – such as gold, silver, copper and mercury – but these materials cannot be removed easily by machines. Instead, large quantities of e-waste are shipped to LEDCs, where people dismantle the equipment by hand. There is evidence that this is damaging both to the environment and to the health of e-waste workers (see page 37).

In LEDCs, e-waste is recycled by hand. This causes problems for the environment and for the health of e-waste workers.

When fields are irrigated a lot of water is wasted. Most of the water flows into rivers and streams carrying dissolved chemicals with it.

Waste water

Not all the waste we produce goes into the bin or into landfill sites – some goes into our water supply. The waste water from sinks, baths, showers and toilets is known as sewage. In MEDCs, nearly all sewage is treated to remove solid waste and **dissolved** chemicals. The cleaned water is then usually released into streams and rivers, where it eventually flows into the sea. In LEDCs, there are some sewage treatment plants, but most sewage is released untreated, where it pollutes streams, rivers and oceans.

Farming and mining are two other sources of waste water. Huge amounts of water are used worldwide to **irrigate** farm crops. Agriculture uses nearly 70 per cent of all the fresh water that humans use. And in parts of Africa and Asia, irrigation accounts for up to 85–90 per cent of all water use.

Dissolved chemicals

Modern farming involves the use of a great deal of chemicals, such as **fertilisers** and **herbicides** (to get rid of weeds) and **pesticides** (to kill harmful insects). Some of these chemicals dissolve in the water used for irrigation and in natural rainfall. The chemicals are then carried into rivers in **run-off** from the farmland, polluting the water and harming plants and animals nearby. Sometimes, mining waste is also released into streams and rivers. Although this waste is not dangerous to human health, large amounts of dumped sediment can smother and kill many of the plants and animals that live in the river or on the seabed.

PLANET WATCH

» According to the US Environmental Protection Agency, 2 million tonnes of electrical items were discarded in 2005.

» About 1.1 million litres of raw sewage enters the River Ganges, India, every minute. That's enough sewage per minute to fill an Olympic-sized swimming pool.

» Each year, about 450 km³ of wastewater are released into rivers, streams and lakes around the world.

3

WHAT DO WE DO WITH WASTE?

Our rubbish has to be collected and disposed of regularly. Rubbish that is left for a long time begins to rot and smell, especially in hot weather. But where should we put it?

Trouble in Italy

In June 2007, while Europe sweltered in a heatwave, the Italian city of Naples stank to high heaven. Waste was dumped on the streets because the city's rubbish tips were full. Criminal groups had been shipping industrial waste from northern Italy and dumping it illegally in the Naples region to earn money. The waste disposal system had broken down and the government was struggling to cope. Before long, angry citizens began to burn the rubbish heaps, which added thick, choking smoke to the atmosphere.

Earth Data

- There have been problems with waste disposal in Campania, Italy (the region around Naples), for over ten years. A study by the World Health Organisation in 2006 showed that in Campania there has been an increase in deaths from illnesses such as cancer because of this waste.

- Pollution from the waste in Campania may also have affected some foods. Campania is famous for producing mozzarella cheese, using milk from herds of buffaloes. In 2008, hazardous chemicals called **dioxins** were found in milk from some dairies in Campania. All milk from the area is now checked before being used in mozzarella production.

City governments are responsible for regularly collecting and disposing of household waste.

Waste collections

The problems in Naples show just some of the reasons why a waste disposal system needs to run smoothly. When the waste began to rot, bacteria grew and rats and other animals were attracted. The city became a breeding ground for disease.

Waste needs to be collected regularly to stop it decaying in our homes. We usually store waste in bags or bins which are collected by a rubbish truck. Sometimes, these vehicles are fitted with **hydraulic** arms that lift and empty large rubbish bins. All modern rubbish trucks have a compactor. This hydraulic device squashes the waste together. Compacting the waste can greatly reduce the space that it takes up. Compacting is also helpful if the waste is going to a landfill site – uncompacted waste that is piled high can be unstable and is likely to blow around in the wind.

Envac systems

Not all countries collect waste in bags and bins. In some places, waste containers are holes in the ground, and collection trucks are like giant vacuum cleaners that suck the waste out through a pipe.

An extension of this idea is the Envac system, which was first developed in Sweden. Waste is thrown away at a collection point close to a group of houses or sometimes inside a building. The waste goes down a chute to an underground container. At regular intervals, a strong vacuum pump sucks the waste out of the container and along a system of pipes to a central collection point. Here, the waste is compacted and loaded on to trucks for disposal.

Envac, is an enclosed, vacuum-operated method of waste collection. Since it was invented in Sweden in 1961, thousands of systems have been installed worldwide.

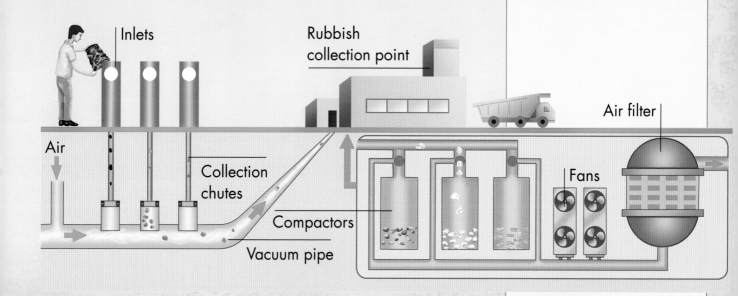

Inlets

Rubbish collection point

Air filter

Air

Collection chutes

Fans

Compactors

Vacuum pipe

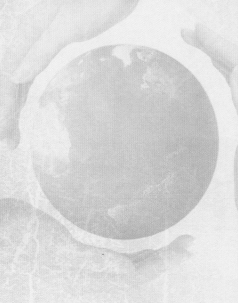

Landfill sites

Once waste has been collected, something has to be done with it. It cannot simply be left lying around. The most popular method of disposing waste is to put it into a landfill site. Landfills can be old quarries, mines or other existing holes in the ground that are filled up with waste.

Before any waste is dumped, the hole is lined with clay and plastic to waterproof it. This is because the food and **organic** waste in the landfill produces slightly acidic liquids as it rots. Rainwater mixes with these liquids to form what are called **leachates**. In a modern landfill site, leachates are collected using drainage pipes and then processed to make them safe.

The rotting organic material in a landfill site also produces a mixture of **methane**, **carbon dioxide** and small amounts of other gases. On some sites, a system is installed to collect landfill gas as it forms. This gas is then burned to generate electricity.

This graph shows the waste disposal methods used in different countries.

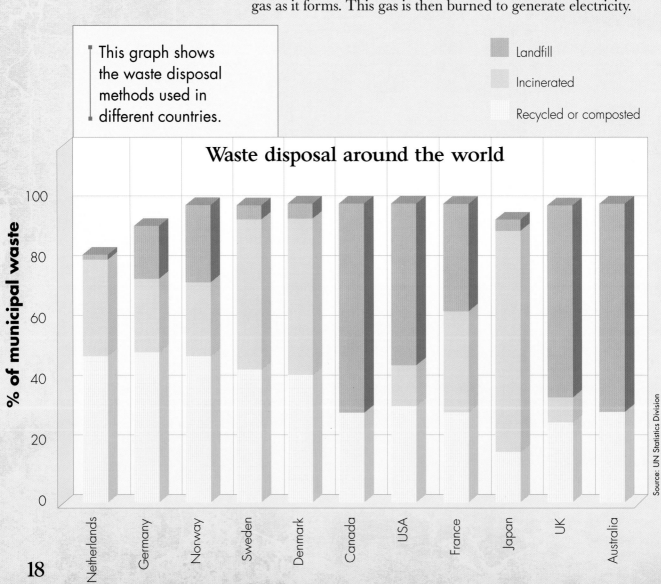

Source: UN Statistics Division

18

A landfill site cannot be used for building because there is no solid rock below the surface – the buildings would sink.

Once the site has been prepared, waste is compacted and dumped in a particular part of the landfill site. When an area is full, it is covered with earth. The landfill is gradually filled up, one area at a time. When the landfill is full, it is covered with another layer of soil. Trees and other plants are grown, and the site often becomes a parkland.

Dumping at sea

Before the 1970s, all kinds of industrial waste and large amounts of oil were dumped at sea. There was also mining waste, sewage, and material that was **dredged** from the seabed in shallow waters, then dumped further out to sea. In 1972, an international agreement known as the London Convention was passed. It reduced the dumping of hazardous waste at sea and banned the dumping of radioactive material.

An improved agreement in 1996 banned the dumping of everything except a few items such as fish waste, dredged material and the solid waste from sewage treatment plants. However, not all countries have signed up to the London Convention and the dumping of hazardous waste at sea still goes on. Dumping of raw sewage in particular is still common in many LEDCs.

PLANET WATCH

» The amount of waste sent to landfill varies between countries. In Australia, nearly 70 per cent of waste goes to landfill, while in the Netherlands it is less than 2 per cent.

» Worldwide, between 21 and 46 million tonnes of landfill gas are produced each year.

» In many LEDCs, an estimated 80–90 per cent of raw sewage is dumped in the sea.

Despite strict laws, a lot of
waste is still illegally dumped
in rivers and streams.

Ocean dumping in history

From the 1920s until 1988, millions of tonnes
of processed sewage from New York and New
Jersey, USA, were dumped in the ocean. In the
summer of 1988, this waste began to cause
problems. Floating waste washed up on many
beaches in the New York area and there were high
levels of disease-causing **microbes** in the water.
There was a public outcry. Dumping sewage at
sea was stopped in New York and later, in 1992,
banned by law across the whole of the USA.

In many other MEDCs, strict laws now also
prevent the dumping of waste at sea. However,
some international companies release harmful
waste in the oceans when they operate in LEDCs.
An enormous pipe off the island of Sumbawa in
Indonesia, for example, releases 145,000 tonnes
of tailings per day into the sea from a mine run
by an international company nearby. The area is
not covered by the strict regulations back home.

Incineration

Incineration means burning waste. Incinerating
waste reduces it to ash, which takes up far less
space than the original waste. Incineration is
popular in countries such as Japan, where there
are few areas that can be used as landfill sites.

Incinerating waste is not like burning wood or
other everyday fuels. The waste is made up of a
huge mixture of materials. When this mixture is
burned, the gas and smoke produced are full of
hazardous chemicals.

Burning the waste at very high temperatures
(over 1,000°C) breaks down the worst of the
pollutants in the incinerator gases. To reach
these high temperatures, the waste moves
through the incinerator on a moving grate,
with air blowing up from below. The oxygen in
this air is essential for the **combustion** process.
The more air that is mixed with the waste, the
stronger it burns.

20

Even with high-temperature incineration, there are still hazardous chemicals in the gases released. Modern incinerators use a range of filters and other devices to remove most of these chemicals. The finest part of the ash produced (**fly ash**) is also full of hazardous chemicals and has to be stored safely. Ash that is safe can be reused for many applications – to build roads, to make cement blocks and as a final covering layer in landfill sites, for example.

Some incinerators make use of the heat they produce to generate electricity or to heat people's homes. The high temperatures can be used to produce steam, which is pumped to nearby homes, a form of 'local heating'. The steam can also be used to power a generator and produce electricity. This kind of incinerator is often called a 'waste to energy plant'.

PLANET WATCH

» More than 4,000 beaches in the USA were closed in 2007 because of sewage pollution.

» Emissions from incinerators have been drastically reduced in recent years. In 1990, for example, one third of all dioxin emissions (see page 42) in Germany came from incineration plants. In 2000, the figure was less than 1 per cent.

Incinerators burn waste at high temperatures. They can be used to generate electricity.

4 EFFECTS OF WASTE DISPOSAL

All waste disposal methods have problems associated with them. This chapter looks at these problems in more detail, and at what effects they can have on the environment.

Earth Data

In many parts of the world, large amounts of untreated sewage are still dumped at sea. This list shows how much (as a percentage) of the total sewage dumped at sea is untreated:

• North Atlantic – 10 per cent
• Mediterranean – 53 per cent
• Latin America and Caribbean – 86 per cent
• East Asia – 89 per cent
• South-east Pacific – 83 per cent

Effects on fresh water

Today, a well-planned, modern landfill site causes few problems to the surrounding environment. However, there are many old landfills still in use around the world. In LEDCs, cities often grow too fast to allow the proper planning of waste disposal. In these cases, landfill sites are simply huge rubbish tips. They may not be managed properly and can pollute the surrounding environment, as well as causing a serious fire hazard.

The Olusosun landfill site in Nigeria is a huge rubbish dump with no safety regulations. Apart from the problem of leaking leachate, there are many fires caused by escaping landfill gas.

Dumping waste in rivers and seas can kill fish and other plants and animals that depend on the water.

In old landfill sites, poisonous leachate often escapes and seeps into underground water, rivers and streams. The acid and chemicals in the water can damage plants, and pass to the animals that eat them. Sometimes, when heavy metals build up in the **food chain**, whole species can be killed off.

Fertilisers that are sprayed on fields can also find their way into freshwater sources. The fertilisers contain nutrients that help plants to grow. When these chemicals get into the water, there is a sudden burst in the growth of water weeds and **algae**. The excessive plant growth clogs up the water and stops sunlight getting below the surface. And when the algae die, bacteria that feed on them use dissolved oxygen in the water to **decompose** the plant material. This reduces the amount of oxygen in the water and has a serious effect on **aquatic** life.

Effects of ocean dumping

Some of the wastes that are released into rivers and streams eventually end up in the sea. For many years, it was thought that the ocean was so vast that wastes dumped there had little effect. However, evidence has shown that waste dumping is extremely harmful to marine environments, especially in coastal regions. A report by the United Nations Environment Programme (UNEP) in 2006 said that about 80 per cent of all ocean pollution is caused by activities on land. Sources of this pollution include sewage plants, power stations, coastal mining, tourist resorts, construction work and run-off water from landfills, farms, mines and cities. It is no longer acceptable to consider the ocean as a huge dumping ground. Our rubbish is putting marine life at huge risk.

Coasts suffer most

The effects of waste pollution are mostly seen around our coasts. Coasts are valuable parts of the ocean where we get most of our fish and large amounts of natural resources. Many people also live on the coast or visit as tourists. The release of untreated sewage, in particular, is affecting coastal areas. Important habitats such as coral reefs, seagrass beds and mangrove swamps are being damaged by raw sewage. In some places, it has caused rapid algae growth. Huge 'blankets' of algae, known as 'algal blooms', can kill thousands of fish by reducing the amount of sunlight and oxygen in the water (see page 23).

Plastics are another major problem in the ocean. It is now illegal to dump solid wastes in the sea in many countries, but huge amounts of plastic still end up in the ocean. The plastic does not rot away like food and other types of organic waste. Instead, it breaks up into pieces known as 'nurdles'. Marine animals often mistake these nurdles for food, which is harmful to their health. Animals can also get tangled or trapped in plastic netting, or in the plastic loops used to hold drinks cans together.

Plastic bags are often eaten by sea turtles because they look like jellyfish. They cause harm because they do not break down like other food.

Many industrial chemicals contain POPs. They are meant to be stored and disposed of safely, but sometimes they leak and cause pollution.

POPs in the atmosphere

Certain chemicals, known as persistent organic pollutants (**POPs**), cause global problems. Some POPs, such as pesticides and industrial chemicals, are waste materials from farms and factories. They are washed into rivers and eventually reach the sea. Other POPs are toxic chemicals produced when materials such as plastics are burned. Dioxins and **furans** are two groups of POPs that are produced during waste incineration. Old incinerators produce large amounts of dioxins and furans. Modern incinerators – using higher temperatures and filters – have greatly reduced the production of these pollutants, but dangerous gases are still being released into the air.

The atmosphere and the oceans are so vast that the POPs we produce are **diluted** to very low levels. However, they can become **concentrated** in the fatty tissues of animals. This is a particular problem in the Arctic. Pollutants are carried northwards on ocean currents from industrialised regions of the USA and western Europe. They are also carried through the air on northbound winds. Levels of POPs can be 70,000 times higher in animal fat tissue than in the oceans and air.

PLANET WATCH

» The biggest collection of waste in the world is not on land, but at sea. The Great Pacific Garbage Patch contains over 3 million tonnes of waste, 80 per cent of which is plastic. The patch is formed by circular currents in the ocean, which concentrate the rubbish in a relatively small area. The waste has been dumped by countries that border the Pacific Ocean.

» Only 5 per cent of the oil polluting the oceans each year comes from oil tanker spills. Over 50 per cent is from drains that run into rivers and the sea, 20 per cent from cleaning tankers at sea and 13 per cent from polluted rainwater. Over 8 per cent comes naturally from the seabed.

Hazardous wastes

Chemical plants, oil refineries and paint manufacturing are few of the many industries that produce hazardous wastes. Millions of tonnes of hazardous wastes are produced every year. Large companies usually treat and dispose of these wastes themselves, but many smaller organisations prefer to pass on their waste to a specialist waste disposal company.

In most countries, there are strict regulations to make sure that hazardous wastes are properly disposed of. It is also illegal to **export** hazardous waste. However, with such large amounts of waste involved, accidents and mistakes do happen. In some cases people try to cut corners to reduce their costs. Invariably, these actions can have effects on human health.

River disaster

Paper manufacturing, for example, uses huge amounts of water, which gets **contaminated** with the chemicals used in the process. Modern paper factories recycle and process the water, so that the waste they eventually produce is no more toxic than treated sewage water. However, in 2003, at a paper mill near Rio de Janeiro, Brazil, a huge tank storing water full of toxic chemicals burst, releasing over 3 billion litres of contaminated water into the Paraiba do Sul river. In addition to killing millions of fish and other living things, the spill affected the water supplies for over 600,000 people.

In 2003, countless dead fish were washed up on Barra beach after toxic waste was released from a paper mill in Minas Gerais state, Brazil.

Countries that use nuclear power take great care over storing and transporting nuclear waste.

PLANET WATCH

» Worldwide, there are over 270,000 tonnes of nuclear waste in storage. About 90 per cent of it is stored in special underwater ponds. A further 12,000 tonnes of waste is created each year.

» Nuclear waste stored underground has multiple layers of protection, including glass or artificial rock, stainless steel and and a watertight material such as clay.

Radioactive materials

One source of waste that needs extremely careful disposal is waste from nuclear power stations. Used nuclear fuel is extremely radioactive, and remains so for a very long time. This waste has to be stored underwater for 40 to 50 years, until it cools down and produces less radioactivity. Even then, the fuel will produce significant amounts of radioactivity for another 10,000 years. In the meantime, it has to be stored safely. Nuclear waste used to be dumped at sea. In 1994 this became illegal, but the radioactive wastes that have already been dumped are still there.

5 FINDING NEW SOLUTIONS

Around the world, waste is piling up faster than we can get rid of it. We need to find better, more environmentally-friendly ways of dealing with this waste.

Earth Data

- Recycling 1,000 kg of aluminium cans saves approximately 5,000 kg of aluminium ore being mined.

- Recycling steel saves about 95 per cent of the energy used to produce steel from metal ores.

- In the USA in 2008, 32.5 per cent of **municipal** waste was recycled.

- In Europe, recycling levels range from about 10 per cent in Greece to 70 per cent in Austria. Australia recycles about 30 per cent and Japan about 17 per cent.

The waste hierarchy

People have begun to develop new ways of dealing with waste. Many of the principles behind these methods can be seen in what we call the 'waste **hierarchy**'. The waste hierarchy has five steps:

- Reduce – the best way to deal with waste is to avoid producing it altogether, or if not, to reduce the amount we produce.
- Reuse – if we cannot avoid a particular type of waste, we can try to reuse it in some way.
- Recycle or **compost** – if we cannot reuse waste, then perhaps we can recycle the materials it is made from. If the waste is food or other organic material we can turn it into compost.
- Produce energy – if waste is not recycled or composted, we can try to get energy from it in some way.
- Dispose – any waste that is left at this stage needs to be disposed of safely.

The waste hierarchy is a useful framework that has become a vital tool in waste management.

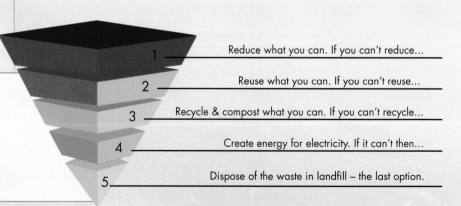

1 — Reduce what you can. If you can't reduce...

2 — Reuse what you can. If you can't reuse...

3 — Recycle & compost what you can. If you can't recycle...

4 — Create energy for electricity. If it can't then...

5 — Dispose of the waste in landfill – the last option.

Reducing waste

The best way to cut down on waste is to avoid making it in the first place. Two ways that households could significantly reduce their waste would be to throw away less food, and to avoid using plastic bags. In the UK, for example, people throw away a third of the food they buy. If people planned their shopping a little more carefully and put more leftovers into garden compost, a lot of this food waste could be avoided.

Worldwide, we throw away over a million plastic bags every minute. Part of the reason that people use so many bags is that they are usually provided by shops for free. Making people pay for plastic carrier bags, and encouraging them to use their own shopping bags, would help to reduce this waste.

In MEDCs, a large part of household waste is packaging. Putting less packaging around products would reduce the amount of waste we generate. Many manufacturers and shops are already beginning to do this, especially for food packaging. New designs of bottles, for example, work just as well with less material. Glass containers use 30 per cent less glass today than they did in 1980. Yoghurt pots that weighed 12 grams in 1980, now weigh only 3 grams.

Reusable 'green' bags are popular among shoppers in Ireland. When plastic bags were taxed in 2002, there was a 94 per cent drop in plastic bag use in a matter of weeks.

Reducing water use

In MEDCs, people can reduce their household water use in simple ways. For example, taking a shower instead of having a bath, and fitting a water-saving device in the toilet cistern, can save up to 700 litres of water per week in a family home. Bigger water savings can be made by collecting rainwater for use in the garden, and by using grey water (water that has already been used for washing) to flush the toilet.

We could make the biggest water savings by reducing the amount of water used for irrigating farm crops. One useful way of reducing irrigation water is to use a method called drip irrigation. In normal irrigation, water is sprayed over a wide area and falls on to crops like rain. Drip irrigation uses far less water because the water is dripped on to the root area of the plants using pipes with small holes along their length. Drip irrigation has been used in MEDCs since the 1960s, but more recently simple, inexpensive drip irrigations systems have been developed for use in LEDCs, too. Saving water this way is crucial for the future, because **climate change** is gradually warming the planet. In the coming years, there will be less water available to use.

Drip irrigation slowly adds water to the soil around the roots of these vines at a rate that's easy to absorb. The water is only used where it is needed.

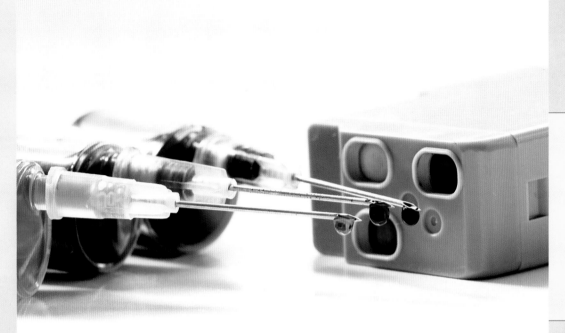

Reuse

Some kinds of waste can be avoided by reusing materials rather than throwing them away. Reuse is different from recycling because, in recycling, the waste material is broken down and re-formed.

Some kinds of packaging can be reused to save waste. One example is using plastic trays instead of cardboard boxes to deliver goods to shops and supermarkets. Bread, for example, can be delivered on standard plastic trays. When the delivery truck brings the bread for that day, the shop will give the driver any empty trays from the previous delivery. These go back to the bakery to be filled again.

Glass bottles can be used again and again in a similar way. In the past, soft drinks and milk were sold in reusable bottles, but in most MEDCs these containers have been replaced by throwaway plastic bottles or cartons. Using refillable bottles could avoid a great deal of waste, if people return the empty containers they have used.

Many expensive items, such as cameras, mobile phones, cookers and fridges, are now thrown away because they are broken or because they are replaced by a newer model. Many items could be repaired, cleaned and re-sold. The US company Caterpillar, for example, has a factory in China that refurbishes tractors and re-sells them.

PLANET WATCH

» In the UK, 360 million plastic bottles were recycled in 2002.

» Recycling a single plastic bottle can conserve enough energy to light a 60 Watt lightbulb for up to 6 hours.

» Of the 44 million laser printer cartridges sold in Europe each year, 74 per cent are used only once.

This car park in California, USA, was made using recycled products.

Re-purposing

Some kinds of waste can be reused for different purposes. For example, construction waste such as broken tiles, bricks and waste concrete can be crushed and turned into **aggregate** – a material used to build roads. Aggregates and non-toxic fly ash from incineration (see page 21) can also be mixed into some kinds of concrete and used as a building material.

Recycling

Recycling materials means breaking them down and re-making them into something new. In MEDCs, the collection of a range of materials for recycling has gradually been increasing in recent decades, but most countries could still do more to save and recycle the materials they use.

A study conducted by the Technical University of Denmark found that in 83 per cent of cases, recycling is the most efficient method to get rid of household waste. Metals, paper and glass are the materials most commonly recycled. Metals such as steel, copper and aluminium can be recycled almost indefinitely, but other materials cannot be recycled more than a few times.

Some kinds of plastic are also recycled. However, there is such a wide range of different plastics that it is not yet possible to recycle them all. Researchers are working on developing new recycling processes for plastic materials.

Sorting materials properly is important for recycling to be successful. In most cases, individuals sort their own waste for recycling, but this is not always done properly. Unsorted materials are often thrown away. One solution to this problem is to use 'single-stream' recycling centres. These recycling facilities can take mixed waste, containing bottles, cans, paper and plastics, and separate the various materials for recycling. Drinks cartons, which contain a mix of cardboard, aluminium foil and plastic are difficult to recycle. In 2008, carton manufacturers and local councils in the UK encouraged the recycling of these cartons. Recycling points were set up around the country and factories were developed that could deal with the separation of paper, plastic and aluminium before recycling.

Composting

Food and other organic waste can be reused by composting it. Any uncooked, plant-based food can be put into a compost heap or bin to decompose. If it is made properly, the heap will turn the waste food into rich compost that can be used to fertilise soil. If people compost food waste at home, this cuts down on the amount of waste that is thrown away. In some places, composting is encouraged on a large scale by local councils. The compost produced by individual households can be sold to help pay for the cost of collecting and processing the waste material.

Magnets, air blowers, and scanners help to separate the various types of waste at this 'single-stream' recycling centre.

PLANET WATCH

» Researchers at Australia's Commonwealth Scientific and Industrial Research Organisation have developed a way to use rubber from car tyres in new materials. The process makes it possible to use tyre waste in a variety of applications, such as shoe soles, car parts, building products and containers for hazardous waste.

Energy from waste

The heat from incinerating waste can be used to produce electricity (see page 21). Most modern incinerators are now designed to heat steam to produce electricity at the same time as burning waste material. Some incinerators are also used to provide heating for local homes and businesses.

The waste in an incinerator produces many polluting gases when it burns. These pollutants have to be trapped and removed, to stop them being released into the atmosphere. An alternative is to make the waste into a fuel first. The fuel will not produce harmful gases when it burns. One way to do this is a process called **pyrolysis**. This involves heating the waste in the absence of oxygen to produce a solid fuel. Another process, called **gasification**, produces gas fuel from the waste material.

Another way of producing fuel gas from waste material is **anaerobic** digestion. This is similar to composting (see page 33) but is done in the absence of air. Microbes break the waste down and produce gas, which can then be used as a fuel. Anaerobic digestion has been used for many years to produce gas from sewage. More recently, new processes allow some kinds of solid waste to be used in digesters instead of sewage.

What is left after reducing, reusing, recycling and producing energy from what we throw away, is truly a waste material. It has to be disposed of safely in a well-prepared landfill site. But if the waste we produce is well-managed, the total waste that we actually throw away should be greatly reduced.

This anaerobic digester turns cattle waste into a gas that can be used as a valuable fuel.

A bottle deposit scheme would have encouraged people to return these glass bottles instead of throwing them away.

A change of attitude

In some parts of the world, effective waste management processes are already in place. In Oregon, USA, for example, a bottle deposit scheme operates whereby people receive five cents for each glass bottle they return to shops. In the UK, supermarkets have set targets for reducing their packaging, and some have already reduced packaging by 25 per cent. Austria recycles about 70 per cent of its waste, and the city of Edmonton, Canada, now manages to recycle or compost over 60 per cent. In addition, Denmark treats 1.1 million tonnes of waste each year by anaerobic digestion.

However, these individual schemes are only scratching the surface of the world's waste problem. While they are a step in the right direction, we need people all over the world to take a completely different attitude to waste. In MEDCs, we have a throwaway culture: if something is old or broken, or even if we are bored with it, we often throw it away. We need to think instead that waste is wasteful. Every time we throw something away, we have to use energy and resources to dispose of it safely. 'Out of sight' is 'out of mind', but this does not cause the problem to go away. The less we throw away, the more energy we save, and the less effect we have on the environment.

PLANET WATCH

Although it is not done on an industrial scale, in LEDCs most materials are reused or recycled in some way. In Senegal, for example:

» Tomato tins are used as drinking cups in rural areas

» Old newspapers and other kinds of paper are used to wrap food bought in the street

» Plastic bags are used to make shoes.

35

6

A GLOBAL CHALLENGE

Waste is a global problem, so the challenge of reducing it depends on us all. Individuals have to take responsibility for reducing their own waste, recycling it and disposing of it.

Exporting the problem

Many governments now pass laws aimed at managing waste more carefully. Recovering and recycling waste has become big business and companies that recycle waste often operate globally. Some cities send their waste to landfill or incineration plants in other parts of the country, or even abroad. Campania in Italy, for example (see page 16), now sends some of its waste to Germany. But moving waste is expensive. It also uses energy and produces **carbon emissions**, which contributes to **global warming**.

(see page 16)

Earth Data

- In 2006, the ship *Probo Koala* tried to unload 500 tonnes of 'slops' (oil waste) for disposal in Amsterdam. However, this unloading was not allowed because there were hazardous materials in the slops.

- The *Probo Koala* then travelled to Abidjan in the Ivory Coast, Africa, where the slops were unloaded and dumped at night. The next day, a stinking cloud of fumes hung over the city and thousands of people were taken ill.

- The oil company that produced the waste tried to make amends by contributing £100 million towards the treatment of the waste dumped in Abidjan.

This barge is taking crushed cars from New York City, USA, to be processed in another part of the country.

On the beaches of India and south-east Asia, old ships are taken apart, often polluting the water.

Ship-breaking

Two types of waste, in particular, are moved around the world: these are ships and e-waste. Ships that have reached the end of their life are usually taken apart in large shipyards. However, in recent years, a huge ship-breaking industry has developed in India, Bangladesh and south-east Asia. Ships are dismantled on beaches – a process that is far cheaper than it would be in organised shipyards. However, the ship-breaking industry is polluting coastal areas. Often, there is also a lack of adequate protective equipment and few health or safety regulations in place to protect workers. They can be exposed to toxic materials left in a ship's holds or oil tanks, and can become ill or injured. Dangerous vapours and fumes from burning materials may also be inhaled. As an alternative to ship-breaking, some ships are now sunk to make artificial reefs.

Exporting e-waste

Large amounts of e-waste are also exported to LEDCs. Here, they are dismantled and valuable materials are removed for recycling. As with ship-breaking, there are no real regulations regarding health and safety in these processes. Recycling is done by hand in scrapyards, often by children. Hazardous chemicals in e-waste include heavy metals such as mercury and cadmium, and dioxins and furans that are released when the plastics are burned. These can cause all kinds of illness among scrapyard workers.

Most of us do not want our junk to be exported to other countries to damage the health of the people living there. It is up to us to make sure that our waste is recycled properly. Checking up on what happens to the materials sent for recycling, and writing to local politicians about problems, are ways of making sure that waste is managed well.

Removing old dangers

The ways that we manage waste today are far better than in the past, and should continue to improve in the future. However, this leaves the problem of the huge amounts of waste that we still have from years gone by. This waste can be very difficult and expensive to clear up. Old mining sites, in particular, are often contaminated with wastes that make the area unsafe for humans. These sites remain abandoned and untreated for many years after the mines close down. In the USA alone, there are over 500,000 abandoned mining sites. About 25,000 of these could cause environmental damage, mostly through water pollution.

Radioactive worries

Even more worrying are the sites of old **uranium** mines and nuclear weapons factories. The amount of this radioactive waste in the USA is staggering. According to estimates by the US Department of Energy, over 3,028 billion litres of **groundwater** – enough to supply 1.5 million homes for a year – remains contaminated with uranium and other toxic chemicals. Another 3,000 million gallons of waste from uranium mines and weapons factories are buried in specially-built landfills. There are likely to be similar amounts of waste from old weapons in Russia, too.

An open-pit uranium mine in France. Making mines like this one safe for the future is a major challenge.

Remediation

Making old mines and other areas safe again is called **remediation**. Traditional remediation techniques include digging up contaminated soil and pumping chemicals through it to draw out the contaminants. Alternatively, groundwater can be pumped from the site, cleaned and put back again. These methods are effective, but slow and expensive.

More recently, researchers have begun to use **bioremediation** for sites full of toxic waste. This involves using plants or microbes to clean up soil and water supplies. A series of reed beds have been used, for example, to clean up water contaminated with mining wastes. Scientists have discovered that some types of fern absorb toxic materials from soil. Most promising is the use of different kinds of bacteria. Some types of bacteria can even clear up radioactive wastes from uranium mining sites.

Making waste safe

Despite the scale of the problem, it is possible to clear up the waste we have produced in the past, and to reduce the amount of waste we generate in the future. New ways of dealing with waste are being developed all the time. In some cases, these ideas are being used together in complete waste management schemes.

However, to really have an effect, waste solutions need to be used worldwide. We can all contribute to making this happen, by cutting down on the waste we produce, and by supporting politicians and organisations that are working to clean up our world. The sooner we act, the sooner we can make a difference.

The fern *Pteris vittata* has been used for bioremediation because it takes up arsenic and other toxic waste from the soil.

PLANET WATCH

» In November 1999, work began to treat waste water at an old mine in County Durham, UK. The water contained high levels of dissolved zinc, which were potentially toxic. The zinc was extremely hard to remove until the University of Newcastle developed a method that used bacteria.

FACTS AND RECORDS

Waste fact file

• In the USA, every week about 570,000 trees are used to produce the Sunday newspapers. Of these, 88 per cent are not recycled.

• In the USA, people throw away 2.5 million plastic bottles every hour.

• A recent USA study found that the production of a computer workstation led to 60 kilograms of factory waste, 27 kilograms more than the weight of the workstation itself.

• Every year some 45,000 tonnes of plastic waste are dumped into the world's oceans. Up to 1 million seabirds and 100,000 sea mammals are killed each year by this plastic waste.

• Around 20 to 50 million tonnes of e-waste are generated worldwide each year. In the USA, some 14 to 20 million computers are thrown away each year. In the EU, the volume of e-waste is expected to increase by 3 to 5 per cent a year. LEDCs are expected to triple their output of e-waste by 2010.

12 tips for reducing waste

1. Avoid buying goods with lots of unnecessary packaging.
2. Buy 'loose food' instead of packaged food where possible.
3. Buy products with refillable containers as much as possible.
4. Buy milk from your milkman using returnable glass bottles.
5. Use your local recycling scheme, if you have one, to recycle as much waste as possible.
6. Choose products made from recycled materials.
7. Avoid using carrier bags: take along your own bags when you go shopping.
8. Avoid buying disposable products such as throw-away cameras, paper handkerchiefs and napkins, or disposable cups.
9. Avoid disposable batteries - use rechargeable ones.
10. Hire videos and DVDs, and borrow books from a library rather than buying them.
11. Sell or donate goods instead of throwing them out.
12. Compost garden waste and kitchen scraps. If there's no room for a compost pile, offer compostable materials to community composting programmes or garden projects nearby.

Waste generated by countries of the world

Country	Waste generated (thousand tonnes)		
	1980	1995	2005
Australia	10,000	*	13,200
Belgium	2,763	4,615	4,847
Denmark	2,046	2,960	3,990
Greece	2,500	3,200	4,853
Ireland	640	1,848	3,050
Italy	14,041	25,780	31,677
Japan	43,995	50,694	51,607
Netherlands	7,050	8,469	10,178
New Zealand	880	1,431	1,541
Norway	1,700	2,722	3,498
Poland	10,055	10,985	9,354
Turkey	12,000	27,234	31,352
United Kingdom	*	28,900	35,077
United States	137,568	193,869	222,863

* No data

Composition of waste

These pie charts show the different make-up of household waste from countries with a low income (LEDCs), countries with a medium income, and high-income countries (MEDCs).

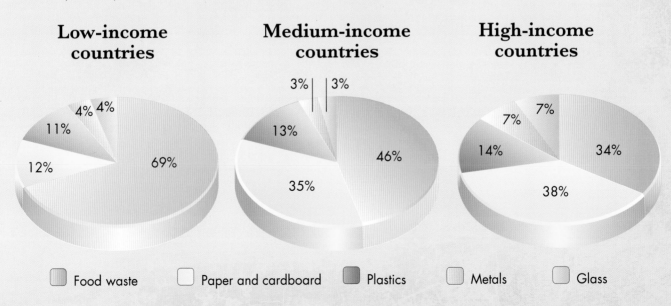

Low-income countries | Medium-income countries | High-income countries

Food waste · Paper and cardboard · Plastics · Metals · Glass

GLOSSARY

aggregate
pieces of crushed stone used in construction

algae
microscopic plant-like creatures found in water

anaerobic
without air

aquatic
in water

bioremediation
repairing damage to the environment by using plants or microbes to clean up soil and water supplies

carbon dioxide
a gas made up of carbon and oxygen, that is found in the air

carbon emissions
gases containing carbon, released when a fuel is burned, for example

climate change
changes in the normal pattern of weather. Today, climate change usually refers to the warming of the world's climate because of a build-up of pollutants in the air

combustion
burning

commercial waste
waste from offices, shops and other businesses, but not large factories

composting
to make compost (a material that can be used to enrich the soil). Compost is made from plant material such as garden trimmings and food leftovers

concentrated
when a substance is increased in strength by removing water (or another substance)

construction
the process of making a building

contaminated
describing something that has been made impure or harmful, often as a result of pollution

decompose
to break down or rot

diluted
when a substance is reduced in strength by adding water (or another substance)

dioxin
a chemical released into the atmosphere when certain substances burn, which can cause pollution and damage to human health

dissolve
to make into a liquid

dredged
dug up from the river or seabed

export
to send goods to another country for selling

fertiliser
chemicals or other substances that enrich the soil and help plants to grow

flammable
easily catches fire

fly ash
a fine ash produced when fuel or solid waste is burned

food chain
the connection between living things in a habitat where one living thing is food for another

furan
a polluting chemical sometimes found in the atmosphere that can damage human health

gasification
a process that converts waste material into a gas by reacting it at high temperatures with controlled levels of oxygen

global warming
the gradual warming of the Earth's climate

groundwater
water found below ground in layers of porous rock called aquifers

herbicide
a chemical used to kill weeds

hierarchy
a system of ordering people or things in which some things are at the top and others are below them

hydraulic
powered by liquid under pressure

infectious
describing someone or something that can pass a disease or illness to another person

irrigate
to supply crops or plants with water so that they grow in a climate that would normally be too dry

landfill site
an area of land set aside as a place where rubbish can be buried

leachate
a liquid produced when food and organic waste rots in a landfill site

LEDCs
short for less economically developed countries, or the poorer countries of the world

MEDCs
short for more economically developed countries, or the richer countries of the world

methane
a gas made from carbon and hydrogen that is a good fuel. Natural gas is nearly pure methane

microbes
tiny living things too small to see without a microscope

municipal
to do with the government of a town or city

ore
rocks rich in metals or other minerals

organic
describing animal or plant material

pesticide
a chemical used to kill insects and other pests that damage farm crops or garden plants

pollution
poisonous or harmful substances in the soil, water or air cause pollution

POPs
persistent organic pollutants. Chemical substances in the environment that do not decompose. POPs can be a damage to human health and the environment

pyrolysis
a process that converts waste material into a solid fuel by heating it in the absence of oxygen

radioactive
giving out dangerous or harmful radiation

remediation
the curing of a problem. Environmental remediation removes pollution or contamination from an environment

run-off
water or other liquid that runs off fields or other ground without soaking in

sewage
the watery waste from bathrooms, kitchens and toilets

tailings
the waste material left behind when the metal or other material has been removed from an ore

toxic
poisonous or harmful to human health

uranium
a kind of heavy metal that is radioactive

FURTHER READING

- *Gorgeous Gifts: Use Recycled Materials to Make Cool Crafts* by Rebecca Craig (Kingfisher Books, 2007)
- *Green Files: Waste and Recycling* by Steve Parker (Heinemann Library, 2004)
- *Sustainable Futures: Waste, Recycling and Reuse* by Sally Morgan (Evans Brothers, 2005)
- *Waste and Recycling (Can the Earth Cope)* by Louise Spillsbury (Wayland, 2008)

INDEX

WEBFINDER

http://www.epa.gov/epawaste/index.htm
Make less waste and protect the planet! This website has activities and games to help you along

www.wasteonline.org.uk
This website from the charity Waste Watch has all kinds of information and wacky facts about waste

http://maps.grida.no/theme/waste
Information about waste presented in graphs and maps from the United Nations

www.recyclezone.org.uk/home_fz.aspx
Check out these recycling games

http://science.howstuffworks.com/recycling.htm
Find out just what happens to all the stuff we put in recycling bins

http://channel.nationalgeographic.com/channel/human-footprint/
A National Geographic feature about just how much stuff each of us uses in a lifetime